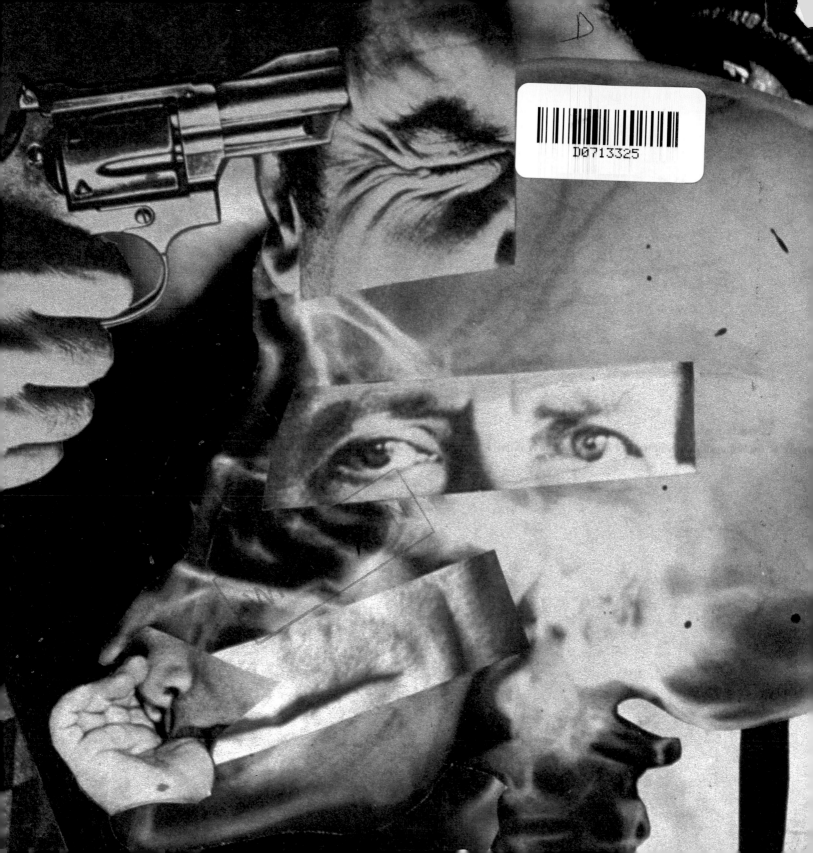

Karen Knorr
Ingrid Pollard
Chris Riddell
Gerald Scarfe
Spitting Image
Ralph Steadman
Trog (Wally Fawkes)
Bill Woodrow

Foreword

The opportunity to make *The Cutting Edge* exhibition was presented to us by the staging of the major retrospective of John Heartfield's work (organised by the Akademie der Künste of the former East Berlin), which is being shown concurrently at Barbican Art Gallery. Heartfield has long been recognised for his innovatory approach, particularly in photomontage, where his manipulation and juxtaposition of images and texts created many powerful and memorable images, decrying the inhumanity of fascism and National Socialism in Germany prior to the Second World War, and making him one of the most strident commentators in the visual arts of the twentieth century. Acknowledging Heartfield's importance, we decided to use the occasion of this retrospective to consider his legacy and the relevance he has had for artists in Britain in recent years.

Rather than consider only the work of artists who are directly indebted to Heartfield, we chose to look more widely and to focus on the many differing ways of working that are current and the interplay between art and society in the broadest of terms. A concern for politics was only one of the criteria which was brought to bear on our choice; there are many artists whose work we would otherwise have liked to have shown, and we do not pretend that this exhibition is a survey of work that touches alone upon political debate nor could we expect to achieve that in one relatively small exhibition. To limit the field, one of the factors which we allowed to direct our choice and that comes into play in the works shown, is a use of irony and satire – tools very familiar to Heartfield.

The Cutting Edge, therefore, displays the work of a small but diverse group of British contributors whose work reflects with wit, satire, and humour upon our current society and its cultural and political events. Some of the artists shown reveal an abiding legacy to Heartfield, both in his pioneering photomontage technique and in his satirical approach as a 'cutting' political critic who used visual means to communicate a message. Moving from light humour to serious political comment and more poetic refrences to the folly of mankind, the exhibition shows the range of British satire with one aspect common to all contributors – the ability to cut through cant and hypocrisy to reach underlying truths by visual means.

We wish to acknowledge with thanks all those who have most generously given their time and helped us form the exhibition. From the outset we were particularly keen to represent the work of cartoonists, illustrators, and animators alongside that of fine artists, and in this respect we are most grateful to the following for their specialist advice: Amanda-Jane Doran of the Punch Archive, Paul Gravett of the Cartoon Art Trust, and Paul Nixon of the Barbican Centre, who have supported the inclusion of cartoonists with great enthusiasm; also Irene Kotlarz and Clare Wilford of the International Animation Festival, and especially Jayne Pilling and Karen Alexander of the The British Film Institute, who advised us from the outset in our plans for a programme of animation, which they also compiled on our behalf. The expertise of these individuals in areas which are relatively new to us has contributed greatly towards the exhibition.

We wish to thank all those who have with great generosity lent works to the exhibition, and would also like to extend our thanks to the Cartoon Gallery, Peter Fluck, Anatol Orient, *Private Eye* magazine, Bonnie Rubenstein of the Lisson Gallery, and Octavia Wiseman of Abner Stein, for all their co-operation. We are also most grateful to Central TV for supporting the Spitting Image presentation, and to W Photo & W Business Presentations Limited for their assistance with the exhibition.

Our thanks go above all to the participating artists, each of whom has assisted us greatly with every aspect of the exhibition. We have enjoyed working with them and are delighted to be able to show their work at Barbican Art Gallery. We are also extremely grateful to the artists for their willingness to contribute towards the catalogue and for being prepared to consider the questions we put to them, which are printed here with their responses. Some of the artists referred directly to the questions while others preferred to make a short statement. Our hope was to touch upon the diversity of approach of the artists we had chosen, feeling that the particular context in which we had placed their work should not override their individual concerns, and their comments make an illuminating addition to the exhibition as a whole.

John Hoole
Curator
Barbican Art Gallery

Carol Brown
Senior Exhibition Organiser
Barbican Art Gallery

The questions

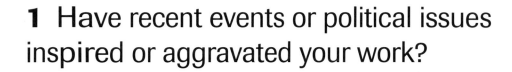

1 Have recent events or political issues inspired or aggravated your work?

2 Commenting on John Heartfield's photomontages, Hans Hess wrote: "Wit is itself the prerunner of montage: every joke that has been told is a montage".* What function does irony or humour have in your work?

3 "John Heartfield used the imagery of the myth to destroy the myth",* how much does your work seek to destroy/expose myths?

4 How important is it to you that the audience acts/reacts upon encountering your work?

* from a lecture given at the ICA, London, 4 November 1969

Spitting Image

1 Spitting Image has to be topical – the most effective caricature always is.

2 Yes we do go for laughs!
Oxford Dictionary definition:

> CARICATURE (noun)
> a) In art. Grotesque or ludicrous representation of persons or things by exaggeration of their most characteristic and striking features.
> b) A portrait or other artistic representation in which the characteristic features of the original are exaggerated with ludicrous effect.

> CARICATURE (verb)
> a) To make a grotesque likeness of.
> b) To burlesque.

3 What the caricaturist trys to do is make us take a closer look. If he or she has succeeded, we then begin to see the victim as a ridiculous creature. And after that, there's not really a lot the poor victim can do. He wears his own caricature wherever he goes. And he or she often begins to resemble the caricature more and more.

4 If you look at a photograph of Mrs Thatcher, she looks like a typical Anglo-Saxon suburban housewife. The *Spitting Image* Mrs Thatcher bears very little visual resemblance to her. But it tells you quite a lot about the character of the ex-Prime Minister.

Or if we look at John Major, we see a rather hesitant, pleasant, not unattractive middle-aged male. But when we see the *Spitting Image* puppet of John Major, we see a character about as interesting as a single coat of grey emulsion. And in fact, the puppet appears grey at all times.

Both of these interpretations must contain at least a tiny germ of truth, otherwise we'd all be wasting our time. And in our case, the viewers would simply not recognise the puppets.

It's this recognition factor which is crucial.

144 (detail) Luck and Law,
photograph of model made for
Sunday Times Magazine 8 February
1981

144 opposite, After Gilray's 'The Plumb Pudding in danger, or State Epicures taking un petit souper', depicting William Pitt and Napoleon carving up the world, 1989
Photograph of model made for cover of a book of poetry never published 'celebrating' 10 years of Thatcher
144 below, Photograph of model made for cover of Private Eye magazine, General Election issue, April 1992

Steve Bell

1 Oh Yes! Especially the rise of John Major.

2 Oh Yes! If I took away the irony and the humour there wouldn't be a great deal of my work left. Oh No!

3 Oh Yes! I'd go along with that. I use the imagery of myth to expose myth quite a not inconsiderable amount really.

4 Oh Yes! Remarkably important.

1 Have recent events or political issues inspired or aggravated your work?

2 Commenting on John Heartfield's photomontages, Hans Hess wrote: "Wit is itself the prerunner of montage: every joke that has been told is a montage".* What function does irony or humour have in your work?

3 "John Heartfield used the imagery of the myth to destroy the myth"*, how much does your work seek to destroy/expose myths?

4 How important is it to you that the audience acts/reacts upon encountering your work?

7 opposite *I Vow to Thee My Country*
3 June 1988
8 below *Botha as Julius Streicher*
13 June 1988

Stephen Dixon

1 Have recent events or political issues inspired or aggravated your work?

2 Commenting on John Heartfield's photomontages, Hans Hess wrote: 'Wit is itself the prerunner of montage: every joke that has been told is a montage." * What function does irony or humour have in your work?

3 "John Heartfield used the imagery of the myth to destroy the myth"*, how much does your work seek to destroy/expose myths?

4 How important is it to you that the audience acts/reacts upon encountering your work?

1 Very much so. Each of the pieces on show was begun as a reaction to a major political event, from the collapse of Soviet Communism (*Second Hand Dreams, The City Rises*) through the Gulf War (*Venus and Mars, On the Brink*) to the fall of Margaret Thatcher and election of John Major (*Death of the Lion Queen, Five More Years*). These pieces seek not to illustrate a particular issue or event, but to point-up alternative (albeit highly subjective) attitudes, opinions, fears and 'truths'. To take an obvious example, we all know that economic self interest was the prime motivation behind 'Operation Desert Storm', yet we allow ourselves to see it as a morally justifiable action in defence of International Law. My work seeks to explore this curious area between what we intuitively (and often cynically) understand, and what we are required to accept as historical fact.

There is, in fact, a long and rich historical tradition of commentary on contemporary social and political events through the ceramic medium.

2 Humour is one of the fundamental ingredients of these recent works. Working in such a narrative tradition, I find that humour, allegory and metaphor are all vital to my visual vocabulary. These are all ways of telling stories in an indirect, even subversive manner; a manner which seeks to draw the viewer in, setting a puzzle to be solved from an arrangement of visual clues. These clues may be historical, traditional, or political, but all are drawn from a common cultural alphabet of images.

In *Death of the Lion Queen*, for example, if one can easily accept that the lion image represents Britain (and historically Establishment and Empire) then only a small step leads to the identification of the Lion Queen as Margaret Thatcher, and another step leads one to see the supporting elephant as Republican U.S.A., her staunchest ally. The humour enters (hopefully) in the relationship between these participants: on closer inspection the lion is found to be a 'lion in sheep's clothing', and in fact represents Geoffrey Howe. (To spell it out, an earlier political attack by Howe had been likened to being 'savaged by a dead sheep', yet it was Howe's speech on Europe that delivered the *coup-de-grâce* to Thatcher's term of leadership – a cruel irony indeed!)

3 Only in the sense that many of our political values and social certainties may be regarded as myths. I would suggest that such contemporary myths as equality of opportunity, faith in justice, and the sanctity of state secrecy, require examination and exposure.

4 It is important to me that the audience engages in a dialogue with my work. It would, however, be ridiculous to imagine that any ceramic object could fundamentally change the opinions and allegiances of an audience, and I would not expect universal agreement with the attitudes of a particular piece. Nevertheless, I believe that it is an important role of the artist (whether in the Literary, Cinematic or Visual Arts) to communicate a personal and independent philosophy, based on an attempt to make sense of the society and environment in which we live.

THE LION QUEEN.

Trog (Wally Fawkes)

The ephemeral nature of the political cartoon is, for me, best summed up in three stages. Stage one: getting the idea, drawing it and standing back for the reaction. Stage two: nobody mentions it, and stage three: if they do, and say 'Great cartoon on Sunday' I can never remember which one it was.

4 How important is it to you that the audience acts/reacts upon encountering your work?

3 "John Heartfield used the imagery of the myth to destroy the myth"*, how much does your work seek to destroy/expose myths?

2 Commenting on John Heartfield's photomontages, Hans Hess wrote: "Wit is itself the prerunner of montage: every joke that has been told is a montage".* What function does irony or humour have in your work?

1 Have recent events or political issues inspired or aggravated your work?

Peter Brookes

1 Have recent events or political issues inspired or aggravated your work?

2 Commenting on John Heartfield's photomontages, Hans Hess wrote: "Wit is itself the prerunner of montage: every joke that has been told is a montage". * What function does irony or humour have in your work?

3 "John Heartfield used the imagery of the myth to destroy the myth"*, how much does your work seek to destroy/expose myths?

4 How important is it to you that the audience acts/reacts upon encountering your work?

1 The breaching of the Berlin Wall, the Gulf War, the August coup against Gorbachev, are all instances of recent political events which provoked a heightened reaction from me. It was easier to focus an emotional response when the events were so extraordinary.

Conversely, however important the European debate, it is difficult to keep finding visual metaphors for what is a slowly-evolving abstraction.

2 Irony is a dangerous weapon for a newspaper artist. It can backfire. By definition, the intended meaning is masked behind an opposing realisation. There is a consequent risk of being misunderstood which to me is anathema. So I use it sparingly.

I do not try to be humorous in my work. This is not a self-conscious attempt to be taken seriously, more a case of realising that if I strive to be funny then the idea is likely to fall flat. Furthermore, a great many of the subjects are no laughing matter: when should you be funny and when not?

I prefer to aim for a certain kind of wit, and to allow any humour to emerge when appropriate rather than be imposed.

3 John Heartfield confronted the greatest and most concentrated evil of this century and I do not pretend to be engaged on the same level. All the same, there are still myths for any commentator to expose today. For example, who heard any Government spokesman explain that the Gulf War was really about oil and dollars?

But most of the time I react to events without analysing my role in this way. It would be arrogant to proselytize on a daily basis. I am as interested in summarising events visually with wit as I am in exploding myths. A myth is as good as a smile.

4 It is important to me that I get a reaction to my work, otherwise I would be filling space on a newspaper to no effect. I would rather readers understand the point I am making than that they should necessarily agree with it. Pains are taken to achieve this by trying to eliminate all ambiguity and by keeping the drawing as uncluttered and direct as possible.

A *VOLUPTUARY under the horrors of Digestion*

Chris Riddell

As a relatively new political cartoonist, recent events have provided a rich source of inspiration; the end of the Cold War, the moves to European Union, the fall of Margaret Thatcher, and the Gulf War, to mention but a few. David Low, the great cartoonist of the forties, wrote "A political cartoonist...is circumscribed by two conditions, timeliness and topicality". In the last four years topicality has not been a problem, the trick is timeliness. For a cartoon to work in a newspaper, as opposed to on a gallery wall months later, it has to be conceived and executed in a sort of controlled panic. As Low writes, "To comment satirically on (new stories') significance before they have passed from 'topicality' altogether, makes what would otherwise be a pleasant profession into an exacting one".

All political cartoons rely predominantly on irony, but humour is an important ingredient. Political cartoons should be funny. I attempt this visually through facial expressions, postures and composition and rely on captions and context for irony. Often a cartoon works best when it is purely visual. I find an accepted cartoon vocabulary is a help, built up of stock figures such as Death and Scythe, bloated capitalist and cigar, British Lion, Russian bear and so on. And, of course, labels can lend metaphorical significance to anything from a piglet to a toothfairy.

It is important to me that my cartoons provoke a reaction, but primarily that, viewed in context as part of the overall newspaper, they fulfil Low's conditions of timeliness and topicality.

CYNICAL COLORS OF BENETTON.

Gerald Scarfe

1 Have recent events or political issues inspired or aggravated your work?

2 Commenting on John Heartfield's photomontages, Hans Hess wrote: "Wit is itself the prerunner of montage: every joke that has been told is a montage".* What function does irony or humour have in your work?

3 "John Heartfield used the imagery of the myth to destroy the myth"*, how much does your work seek to destroy/expose myths?

4 How important is it to you that the audience acts/reacts upon encountering your work?

132-143 opposite *Ronald Reagan*
below *Mad Cow* from *Who's to
Blame?* c.1988-92

Animation

1 Have recent events or political issues inspired or aggravated your work?

2 Commenting on John Heartfield's photomontages, Hans Hess wrote: "Wit is itself the precurner of montage: every joke that has been told is a montage." * What function does irony or humour have in your work?

3 "John Heartfield used the imagery of the myth to destroy the myth"*, how much does your work seek to destroy/expose myths?

4 How important is it to you that the audience acts/reacts upon encountering your work?

British animation has been making its mark since the 1920s. In the last few years, UK animators have gained an outstanding international reputation, while at home, audience interest and enthusiasm for animation has grown in leaps and bounds.

The work here, most of which is from the British Film Institute's animation collection, is a sample of the most challenging and inventive use of the art of animation in recent years, not just in the range of techniques used: drawn cartoon, model, and live action, amongst others, but also in the issues addressed: incest, the arms war, body image, and the nuclear nightmare. Cartoonists like Christine Roche and Steve Bell have turned their talents to animation; as a means of production it is relatively accessible and provides imaginative opportunitites to explore tough issues.

The majority of work featured in the women's programme comes from the forthcoming Connoisseur Animation home video collection *Wayward Girls and Wicked Women* – three volumes of the best work from women animators. The British work from that collection featured here displays a bold, engaging and playful use of the medium, exploring a variety of subjects from the law to autobiography in sometimes serious, sometimes hilarious ways.

The award-winning Aardman studio of *Creature Comforts* fame have demonstrated just how imaginatively plasticine and model animation can be used, bringing their characters to life via vivid observational detail and idiosyncratic touches of humour. *Babylon,* a large-scale production, centres on a conference for arms dealers.

David Anderson, one of the UK's leading animators, is represented here by two films: *Dreamless Sleep,* a mixture of cel model animation and live action, which is a poignant allegory on the theme of nuclear destruction, while *Door* concerns a man's relentless

and impetuous curiosity and the results of his actions when he takes a step too far.

The contemporary work from British and British-based animators show-cased here, is a testimony to the continuing tradition of innovation, creativity and humour that distinguishes UK animation.

Animators include:
Aardman Animation
David Anderson
Steve Bell
Bob Godfrey
Candy Guard
Maybelle Peters
Sarah Pucill
Joanna Quinn
Marjut Rimmenen
Christine Roche
Karen Watson

from *You be Mother* 1990
by Sarah Pucill

opposite, from *The Stain* 1991 by
Marjut Rimmenen and Christine
Roche
below, from *Door* by David Anderson

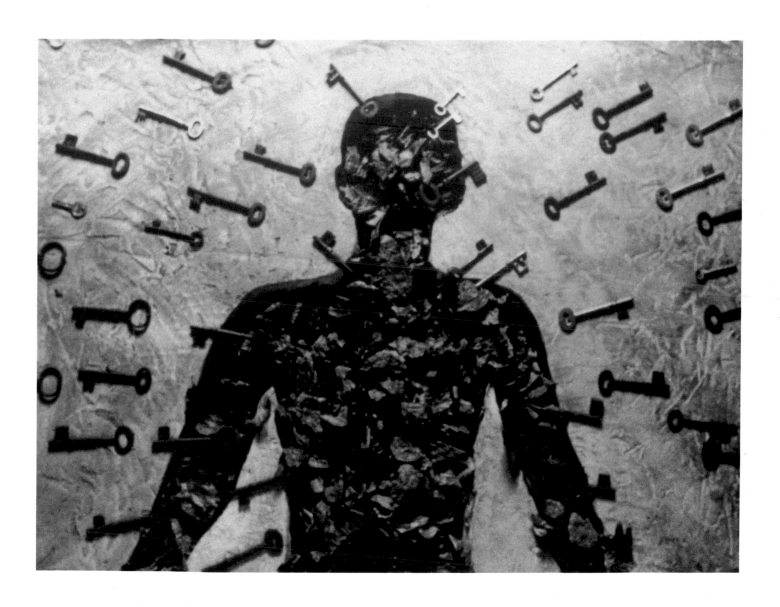

Jacky Fleming

1 Not half!

2 To raise an eyebrow or a laugh. Without it there is no joke.

3 To destroy a myth would be impossible, but a myth exposed is a sheepish sight.

4 Audiences terrify me.

4 How important is it to you that the audience acts/reacts upon encountering your work?

3 "John Heartfield used the imagery of the myth to destroy the myth"*, how much does your work seek to destroy/expose myths?

2 Commenting on John Heartfield's photomontages, Hans Hess wrote: "Wit is itself the prerunner of montage: every joke that has been told is a montage".* What function does irony or humour have in your work?

1 Have recent events or political issues inspired or aggravated your work?

and what are you going to be when you grow up little girl?

HORRIBLE

85–86 opposite and below, from
Be a Bloody Train Driver 1991

I wish these feminists would stop whingeing and do something

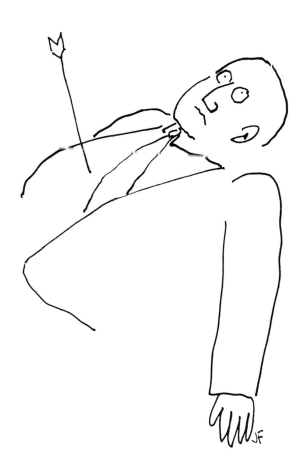

Ralph Steadman

1 Recent domestic politics have inspired only apathy. International politics and the cataclysmic upheavals of recent years have strengthened my stance as a non-partisan observer and commentator on the human condition. It is no longer a matter of right or left, just right or wrong. Maybe we are making a little progress at last. The barriers are down and we are naked. Instead of forcing life into some rigid ideology, we must now use reason and understanding, shed our complacency and mind-numbing arrogance, and ask ourselves how each of us can be of help as fellow travellers through life. Nature herself will finally force us to change, doing what it must to survive, even eliminating us in the process. That might just be the great and heroic challenge of the 21st Century.

2 I don't quite see Hans Hess' point, unless he means that montage is a kaleidoscope of subconscious impulses provoked by chance discoveries of existing material reborn in fresh juxtaposition through the mind, the eye, and the wit of the artist. Now that is the kind of mouthful I can get my teeth into. Irony, particularly, plays a seminal role in my work and humour is a humanising and approachable device which I cannot resist, especially if it is mischievous.

3 In my own work I have found satisfaction in the surprise and the compulsive immediacy of instant replay amongst a disparate selection of conflicting images. Society is waterlogged in a dazzling torrent of media hype, a cornucopia of opulence, wretchedness and banality. Recycling these elements and finding something fresh, provocative and even surprising within its deluge is pure joy – a pandora's box of glitz, bits and pieces. It is probably the nearest thing to being a child again, opening a huge new trunk of unknown toys to manipulate in whichever way you please.

4 It is absolutely vital that an audience responds positively or negatively to my work. Indifference is the enemy to the artist.

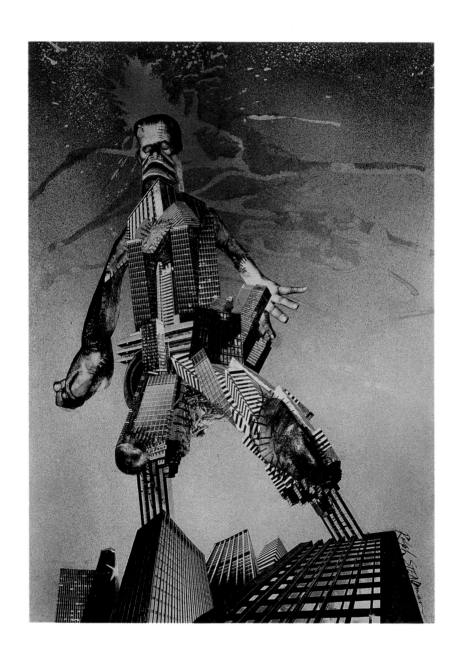

Peter Kennard

1 Have recent events or political issues inspired or aggravated your work?

2 Commenting on John Heartfield's photomontages, Hans Hess wrote: "Wit is itself the prerunner of montage: every joke that has been told is a montage"." What function does irony or humour have in your work?

3 "John Heartfield used the imagery of the myth to destroy the myth"*, how much does your work seek to destroy/expose myths?

4 How important is it to you that the audience acts/reacts upon encountering your work?

When I was at the Slade in the late sixties the orthodoxies of Modernism were still being perpetrated. Modern Art was a bus driven by Cezanne with Matisse as the conductor and Jackson Pollock as the drunken passenger. Clement Greenberg was the inspector whose eye you tried to avoid as he came up the aisle in case you'd bought the wrong ticket. On leaving the Slade this was the only bus to get on and if you didn't make it you would wait at the bus-stop forever. As novelist Ken Kesey said at the time, in a different context, "you were either on the bus or you were off". An even worse fate was to enter one of those buses driven by foreign 'Marxists', who would drive you away from the womb of Artland WC1 into a land of grey basements and 'ordinary' people, definitely a wrong turning. Against the odds, to find a way to relate my growing political commitment to my art, I got on the wrong bus and found the driver was John Heartfield. His work was distinctly off limits in England at the time and hardly appeared in official histories of Modern Art.

His work developed from fragmentary collages into carefully constructed photomontages that not only reported on the rise of Fascism but became a tool in the struggle against Fascism. By connecting two clicks of the camera shutter he could create a third meaning that would make invisible connections visible.

Heartfield developed a form that could intervene in events and balance on the knife-edge between art and life. It is this artless quality about photomontage which led me away from painting. Looking at a painting of war the viewer immediately relates the image back to other paintings of war. A photo-montage, however, takes the viewer back to the war, the subject portrayed. To many people it might not appear to be art at all, and a bloody good thing too.

In 1983, a photomontage I had produced for CND was copied by a right wing pressure group, The Coalition For Peace Through Security, in one of their pamphlets. CND asked me to take them to the High Court on the grounds of copyright infringement. The Coalition's defence led by Douglas Hogg, MP, questioned whether it was an 'artistic work' within the meaning of the Copyright Act.

It was stated that the interweaving of two images in my photomontage was not the result of enough mental effort to constitute a work of art. A farcical debate ensued about what did constitute a work of art. We lost, but the example shows how photo-montage through its use of familiar imagery can by-pass what is normally thought of as art. If I'd made a painting of the same subject there would have been no question that this was a work of art.

Today, artists all over the world are looking for methods to rip apart the smooth veil covering official lies, to make work that can equate the price of weapons and affluence with the fact of poverty, starvation and the planet's destruction. There are more images that reveal less than ever before.

How can we 'picture' the Disappeared – people who are torn from their houses at night and rendered invisible by authoritarian regimes? Does the image of a defence minister on TV show that the Social Services are being destroyed in our country to pay for weapons intended to destroy the people of another? What does a photograph of a nuclear power station tell us? Not that its radioactive emissions can cause birth deformities. Finally, where were the arms dealers in those photographs of the destruction on the road to Basra? Heartfield would have montaged them in. His method of taking easily recognisable images and through juxtaposition rendering them unacceptable is even more relevant today.

From the article 'Piecing together the truth', first published in *The Guardian* 26 March 1990.

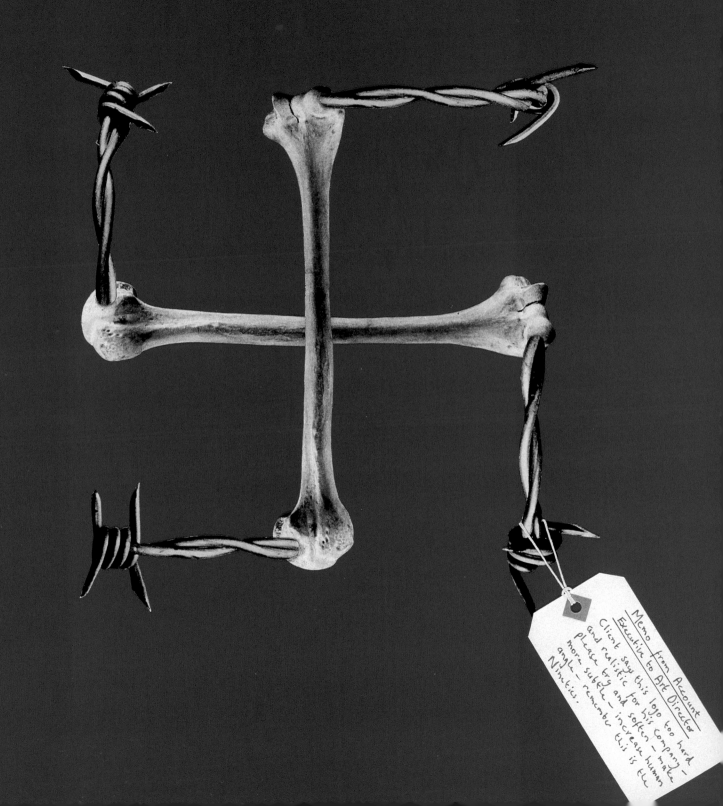

105 (detail) opposite *Memo*
pub. *Weekend Guardian* 30-31 May
1992
105 (detail) right *Defended to Death*
1983
cover for the book of the same title

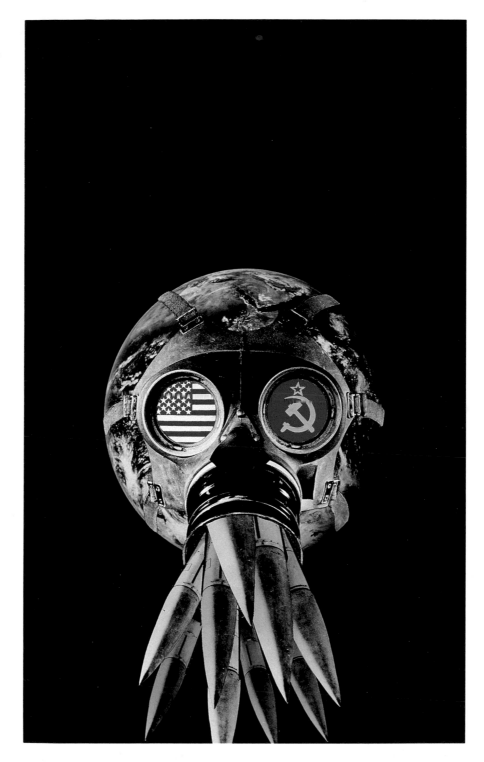

Ingrid Pollard

1 My work is less concerned with immediate events than with wider issues, but politics does, of course, feed into it. Much of my work looks at Englishness and representation. It concerns what exists already rather than the next political moment, and is more about identity and how that is constructed by society. I draw from my own personal history and relate that to, or use it to speak about broader themes. Over the last eight years personal issues have become increasingly important.

2 In the work included here, there is a humorous element, but depending upon who you are, you don't know whether to laugh or not when presented with images that traditionally have been used to re-inforce a stereotype. I like the audience to be a bit uncomfortable. I am trying to touch the subconscious ideas that people have about others and draw upon negative aspects in order to look at these ideas in a different way. Perhaps I tap into nervous laughter. When pressed, some reactionary views come out. I am wary, however, of trivialising a subject by using humour, though it can be a useful tool to encourage an engagement with my work.

Irony has a strong role which comes into play through the use of language. I quote from tourist information brochures or a passer-by's comments. The text is normally used to set off the picture: the image might be pleasant, a beautiful landscape for example, while the words might convey something contradictory. A seemingly innocent phrase can take on another identity and a different kind of resonance by the juxtaposition, and a third, new meaning is formed from the combination of two.

I made this particular work in Hastings not only because it has all the qualities of a typical English seaside town, but also because of its historical associations. It also has a language school, so you are likely to hear French and German and, being close to

London, there are always visitors from urban areas.

Beacause of the Norman Conquest, Hastings provokes thoughts of invasion and repulsion. It is still a place which is invaded. I imagine the people who live there must get annoyed by the tourists, yet they make their living out of them, just as in other seaside resorts, though the sense of history gives an added depth of meaning.

3 One myth I deal with is that black people only exist in an urban setting, or if not there then in the Caribbean or the jungle. Another is the manufactured myth of the countryside idyll. I set up a dialogue between the two myths and so ask, for example, who does the land belong to? I also try to counter the way that landscape is depicted in photography, i.e. with hardly anyone in it. In my photographs the person is central, dominating the horizon or piece of land. That black people are recognised in this way is just the tip of the iceberg. It is a metaphor through which I question the nature of Englishness itself.

4 I hope that my work does set up something – a thought process that questions ideas that are taken in unconsciously and the assumptions people make. The elements in my pictures are usually understood, yet people often go away with ideas that are very different from what I had intended. That is inevitable; we are all individuals with our own histories. But I hope that the memory of my work will return when people look at other images and play a part in dismantling prejudice.

From a conversation with Ingrid Pollard, June 1992

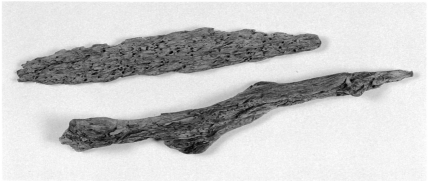

... "... *and what part of Africa do you come from?*"
inquired the walker...

See England under my rule

Karen Knorr

1 Political issues related to class, gender, race, and income distribution in the first world, have inspired and informed my work for over ten years.

Although Major seeks a classless society based on meritocratic principles, nevertheless, there is not enough change in the corridors of power. Take, for example, the issue of gender. Do the proportion of women MPs reflect the voting population? How many black company directors are there? What sex are most principal lecturers in higher education? The Labour Party does not come out of this smelling like roses.

After the Big Bang and deregulation, why hasn't there been an effective regulatory body set up to monitor the city's procedures? The head of IMRO has gallantly taken responsibility for errors concerning pension funds and the Maxwell scandal. He should not be the only one. Too many abuses of the system are taking place. Blue Arrow, Guinness, B.C.C.I., and more recently the Maxwell scandal, harmed many people's lives.

These events could not but effect the making of my most recent work *Capital*.

The earlier work *Connoisseurs* completed in 1989 (started in 1986) refers to connoisseurship in the arts and the heritage industry, which during the 'boom' years led to excesses in the secondary art market and culminated in the sale of Van Gogh's sunflowers. It also parodies those 'master discourses' which serve to legitimize art collecting and the conflicting correct views on the arts.

2 Irony and humour in my work are devices employed to enable viewers to make up their minds for themselves about the attitudes described.

Irony, the main figure deployed, is notoriously difficult to stabilize and risks being taken literally. That is why context is very important to the work. It is also the reason I work in series so that there are different levels of humour operative in the relationship between the images and texts.

3 Myths are very powerful. All of us relate to the world around us in terms of representations, stories and accounts offered to us by the media, the biggest myth-makers of today, particularly advertising and the cinema. None of us can be outside these myths nor can we ever entirely shatter or expose them since they have a tendency to become part of our very own identities. Mickey Mouse, Denis the Menace, and Catwoman, are comic strip characters that I have had meaningful relationships with. They were characters that I grew up with as a child. Today's children look up to Ninja Turtles and Michael Jackson. Myths can offer positive and empowering role models but they can also be used to smooth over contradictions and make reality more acceptable. These are the ones that I seek to describe. I fear that they can not be destroyed by art alone but that education is the place where this exposure can really take place.

4 The intention of my work is to make people think. That would be action enough.

113 opposite *Liquid Assets* 1991
from *Capital*
111 below *The End of History* 1992
from *Capital*

Art & Language

1 Such questions tend to stun the mind. They seem to demand something so laconic as to be meaningless: 'Of course, what would you expect?'.

What are the boundaries of political events? The only headline event we've specifically recorded is the U.S. bombing of Tripoli. The outrage happened to coincide with our being invited to design a magazine cover. With this exception we have not been concerned with any 'event' considered from some Artistically Archimedian point outside, but with the mechanisms by which they are described and understood and in which we are unavoidably complicit; the self-images of the age, if you like.

The ideological process of this age of depoliticization and capitalist triumphalism has been identified as Postmodern, and it is in Postmodernism that the present model of human beings as cyphers shorn of (romantic) moral purpose is animated. The Reagan-Thatcher-Kinnock age has brought us a justifying theory of the Western political tradition emptied of its tiny glimpse of humanity. The justifying theory (or story, if you like) of Western political culture incorporates a model of men and women as creatures of appetite, as appropriators of utilities. The argument is that we must build (or have built for us) a society and a political culture which recognizes the possession of these appetites as our human essence and which maximizes their satisfaction. The Postmodernist affirmation is a part of this development in political culture. It is, however, not at all paradoxical that the consequent artistic formula recapitulates the banal essence of socialist realism. The only new thing is multiplicity. The onlooker and the artist are bound by the same conditions. They must be gratefully solipsistic opportunists. The facile celebration of the play of contrasts is the minute self-assertion by which submission to tyranny is masked.

2 Heartfield isn't funny. Hess' ponderous metaphor isn't all that illuminating. Jokes involve displacement, irony is, no doubt, *l'essence du Rire,* etc., etc. Our work is sometimes wittingly funny. It is often, no doubt, unwittingly so. Sometimes it involves jokes. These may or may not be funny. The problem is, as Baudelaire and Paul de Mann suggest, that those who would be ironists usually end up as its victims. The joke is on us. We have a *métier,* but it is a *métier* in which we are acutely uncomfortable.

3 The matter of myth is something of a difficulty. If myth is something like a necessary <u>falsehood</u>, as distinct from a culturally cherished fiction, then its myths that compose the preponderance of our cultural materials. The difficulty is in avoiding the journalistic assumption that myths are destroyed in merely being exposed as falsehoods. Our real work is to make them unworkable. This often involves the exposure of our own complicity in the workings of illusion. If we wish to intervene in the general dreamwork, the first thing we must admit is that we mostly do it in our sleep.

4 We live in the hope that our work will be looked at by someone. To be an onlooker is to act and react in some way. But that is not what you are asking. We set up the trap in the expectation that it will be sprung from time to time. We do not seek to predict the suffering (or the pleasure) of those who get caught. Art and Social Purpose (and its cognates) has always sought to quantify its effects upon a quantified audience. This is entirely misguided. We seek neither the literal-minded penitent nor those who would wish to be our boon companion. Perhaps we seek those who know the absurdity of both these possibilities. They might talk to us, we might learn something.

We aim to be amateurs, to act in the unsecular forbidden margins. We shall make a painting in 1995 and call it Hostage; A Roadsign Near the Overthorpe Turn. The work will be executed in oil on canvas. It will measure 60 cm. x 40 cm. The white roadsign will occupy about half the picture. It tells us we are 7 miles from Brackley, 2 from Overthorpe and 2 from Warkworth. These names will be scarcely visible in a tangle of lines. The professional may cast a colonising eye, but the tangle will go to a corporeal convulsion beyond her power. The painting will be homely and priggish. We may hide behind our speech at this appalling moment.

5 opposite *Hostage XLVI* 1990
6 right *Hostage XLVIII* 1990

Bill Woodrow

The *Ship of Fools* is an ongoing series of sculpture first started in 1984. *Endeavour* is the tenth and most recent. It differs significantly from the previous sculptures in the series, in that it does not utilise the image of a sailing ship, but purports to be an artifact dredged from the first wreck of the *Ship of Fools*.

See also Lynne Cooke's text in *Parkett* no. 12, 1987

4 How important is it to you that the audience acts/reacts upon encountering your work?

3 "John Heartfield used the imagery of the myth to destroy the myth"*, how much does your work seek to destroy/expose myths?

2 Commenting on John Heartfield's photomontages, Hans Hess wrote: "Wit is itself the prerunner of montage: every joke that has been told is a montage".* What function does irony or humour have in your work?

1 Have recent events or political issues inspired or aggravated your work?

171 *Endeavour (cannon dredged
from the first wreck of the Ship of
Fools)* 1990
opposite and previous page, details

Mona Hatoum

1 Have recent events or political issues inspired or aggravated your work?

2 Commenting on John Heartfield's photomontages, Hans Hess wrote: "Wit is itself the prerunner of montage: every joke that has been told is a montage".* What function does irony or humour have in your work?

3 "John Heartfield used the imagery of the myth to destroy the myth"*, how much does your work seek to destroy/expose myths?

4 How important is it to you that the audience acts/reacts upon encountering your work?

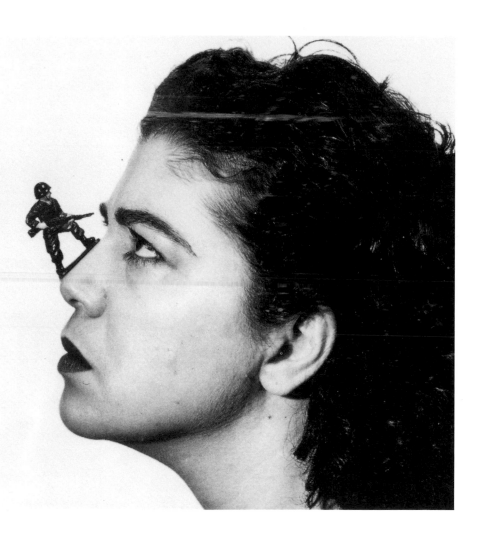

OVER
MY
DEAD
BODY

Fanny Adams

1 Have recent events or political issues inspired or aggravated your work?

2 Commenting on John Heartfield's photomontages, Hans Hess wrote: "Wit is itself the prerunner of montage: every joke that has been told is a montage." What function does irony or humour have in your work?

3 "John Heartfield used the imagery of the myth to destroy the myth'", how much does your work seek to destroy/expose myths?

4 How important is it to you that the audience acts/reacts upon encountering your work?

IN	OUTED
MORISOT SKETCH eight figure saleroom price!	**LISSON GALLERY**
GALLERY CRECHE FACILITIES Peter Palumbo annnounces high priority!	**ANTHONY D'OFFAY**
SHOCK DISCOVERY living women artists located in many U.K. areas!	**NIGEL GREENWOOD**
TURNER PRIZE all woman jury select female winner	**GROB GALLERY**
PRINCESS DI describes D'Offay's as a monstrous carbuncle on the face of a much loved art scene	**EDWARD TOTAH**
U.K. ART SCHOOLS advise employing a token male in all art departments	**RAAB GALLERY**
TRAFFIC ROUNDABOUT DEDICATION women's contribution to the arts acknowledged!	**BERNARD JACOBSON**
TATE GALLERY gives a living British woman artist a retrospective	**MAYOR GALLERY**
BRIAN SEWELL thrown in Atlantic. Nation mourns	**ALBERMARLE GALLERY**
	WADDINGTON

FANNY ADAMS
P.O. BOX 1503, London, SW9 0LQ

THESE GALLERIES SHOWED LESS THAN 15%

WOMEN ARTISTS, OR NONE AT ALL, IN 1991

FANNY ADAMS
PUTS YOU IN THE PICTURE

CRITIC'S CHOICE*

Franceso Clemente Anthony Caro Hamish Fulton Cheri Samba Mark Wallinger Arthur Tress **Cornelia Parker** Blair Hugh-Stanton Willie Doherty Sol Lewitt Jasper Johns **Ana Maria Pacheco** Garry Winogrand Egon Schiele Chris Garnham Anish Kapoor Andrew Serrano Michelangelo Pistoletto Toulouse-Lautrec Mike Bidlo Gerhard Richter Manuel Ocampo Georgio Morandi Hokusai Matthew Studling **Edwina Leapman** Ulrich Rückrlem Richard Long Constable **Karen Knorr** Damien Hurst Martin Disler Richard Artschwager **Cindy Sherman** Lee Friedlander Tony Cragg Allan McCollum Richard Wilson Alexandras Macijanskas Perry Roberts Craig Wood Jack B. Yeats Victor Pasmore Max Ernst **Rachel Budd** Art and Language Tom Wesselman James Hagouin **Fiona Rae** John Virtue Man Ray David Austen Christian Boltanski Werner Bischof Stanley Spencer Thomas Bernstein Franceso Clemente Anthony Caro Hamish Fulton Cheri Samba Mark Wallinger Arthur Tress Willie Doherty Sol Lewitt Jasper Johns **Ana Maria Pacheco** Garry Winogrand Egon Schiele Andrew Serrano Michelangelo Pistoletto Toulouse-Lautrec Mike Bidlo Gerhard Richter Manuel Ocampo Georgio Morandi Hokusai Ulrich Rückrlem Richard Long Constable Damien Hurst Martin Disler Richard Artschwager **Cindy Sherman** Lee Friedlander Tony Cragg Allan McCollum Richard Wilson Perry Roberts Craig Wood Jack B. Yeats Victor Pasmore Max Ernst Art and Language **Fiona Rae** Man Ray Christian Boltanski Werner Bischof Stanley Spencer Thomas Bernstein Franceso Clemente Hamish Fulton Cheri Samba Mark Wallinger Sol Lewitt Jasper Johns **Ana Maria Pacheco** Garry Winogrand Egon Schiele Andrew Serrano Michelangelo Pistoletto Toulouse-Lautrec Mike Bidlo Gerhard Richter Manuel Ocampo Hokusai Ulrich Rückrlem Richard Long Constable Damien Hurst Martin Disler Richard Artschwager **Cindy Sherman** Lee Friedlander Tony Cragg Richard Wilson Perry Roberts Craig Wood Jack B. Yeats Victor Pasmore Max Ernst Man Ray Werner Bischof Stanley Spencer Franceso Clemente Cheri Samba Mark Wallinger Jasper Johns Ana Maria Pacheco Garry Winogrand Andrew Serrano Toulouse-Lautrec Mike Bidlo Gerhard Richter Manuel Ocampo Richard Long Constable Richard Artschwager **Cindy Sherman** Lee Friedlander Richard Wilson Craig Wood Jack B. Yeats Max Ernst Man Ray Werner Bischof Stanley Spencer Franceso Clemente Jasper Johns Andrew Serrano Toulouse-Lautrec Mike Bidlo Gerhard Richter Manuel Ocampo Richard Long Constable Richard Artschwager **Cindy Sherman** Richard Wilson Jack B. Yeats Max Ernst Man Ray Werner Bischof Stanley Spencer Andrew Serrano Toulouse-Lautrec Mike Bidlo Gerhard Richter Manuel Ocampo Richard Long Constable Richard Artschwager **Cindy Sherman** Richard Wilson Jack B. Yeats Max Ernst Man Ray Stanley Spencer Andrew Serrano Toulouse-Lautrec Mike Bidlo Gerhard Richter Manuel Ocampo Richard Long Constable Richard Artschwager **Cindy Sherman** Richard Wilson Max Ernst Man Ray Stanley Spencer Toulouse-Lautrec Gerhard Richter Richard Long Constable Richard Artschwager **Cindy Sherman** Richard Wilson Stanley Spencer Toulouse-Lautrec Gerhard Richter Richard Long Constable Richard Artschwager **Cindy Sherman** Richard Wilson Toulouse-Lautrec Gerhard Richter Richard Long Constable **Cindy Sherman** Richard Wilson Gerhard Richter Richard Long Constable **Cindy Sherman Cindy Sherman Cindy Sherman Cindy Sherman Cindy Sherman Cindy Sherman Cindy Sherman Cindy Sherman**

* Every week the art critics of 'Time Out' make their 'Critic's Choice'. This was their selection in 1991. Tokenism still isn't enough ...

FANNY ADAMS
PUTS YOU IN THE PICTURE

Biographies

Selected recent exhibitions and publications
only are listed.

Art & Language

Mel Ramsden, b. 1944, Ilkeston, Derbyshire
Michael Baldwin, b. 1945, Chipping Norton,
Oxfordshire
Both live in Middleton Cheney, Northamptonshire
Exhibited widely in Europe, Australia, New Zealand,
and the United States of America since 1967.

RECENT SOLO EXHIBITIONS
1990   *Hostages XXIV - XXXV*, Marian Goodman
        Gallery, New York
1991   *Hostage Paintings: The Dark Series*, Lisson
        Gallery, London
        Hostage Paintings 1987-1991, ICA, London, and
        tour to John Hansard Gallery, The University,
        Southampton; Arnolfini Gallery, Bristol
        Hostages, Galerie de Paris, Paris
        The British School, Rome
1992   Galerie Isy Brachot, Brussels

PUBLICATIONS
Art & Language have produced many books,
pamphlets, records, articles, essays and reviews since
1967, as well as the following periodicals:
Art-Language, 1969-1985; *Analytical Art*, 1971 & 1972;
The Fox, 1975-76

RECENT PUBLICATIONS ON ART & LANGUAGE INCLUDE:
1990   John Roberts, *Postmodernism, Politics and Art*,
        Manchester University Press
1991   Charles Harrison, *Essays on Art & Language*,
        Basil Blackwell Ltd., Oxford
        Hostages XXV -LXXVI, Lisson Gallery, London,
        Galerie de Paris, Paris; Marian Goodman
        Gallery, New York. Interview by David
        Batchelor, essay by Christian Schlatter

1992   Thomas Dreher, *Konzeptuelle Kunst in
        Amerika und England Zwischen 1963 und
        1976*, Peter Lang, Frankfurt am Main, Bern,
        New York, Paris.
        Art & Language: Now they are, Galerie Isy
        Brachot, Brussels, texts by Paul Wood:
        'Allegories of Identity', and Art & Language:
        'Art & Language paints a picture (VI)' *
        *includes a list of solo exhibitions and
        bibliography in English.

Steve Bell
b. 1951, London
Studied: Teeside College of Art, Middlesbrough; Leeds University (Fine Art), Exeter University (PGCE)
Lives in Brighton
Freelance cartoonist and illustrator since 1977.
Has drawn cartoons and illustrations for periodicals ranging from *Whoppee, Cheeky,* and *Jackpot,* to *New Statesman & Society* and *Social Work Today,* also for the *NME, Time Out,* and *City Limits.* Currently working mainly for *The Guardian,* where he has drawn a daily strip cartoon since November 1981 and now regularly draws large political cartoons. He has made several short animation films with Bob Godfrey for Channel 4 and the BBC, and has recently drawn a strip for BBC2's *Standing Room Only* football programme.

Peter Brookes
b. 1943, Liverpool
Studied: Manchester College of Art and Central School of Art and Design, London
Lives in London
Freelance illustrator since 1970, has taught at Central School of Art and Design, and since 1979 been a Visiting Lecturer at The Royal College of Art, London. Joined *The Times* as Political Cartoonist/Illustrator in 1983.
Exhibited in Britain at The National Theatre, The Victoria and Albert Museum, The Imperial War Museum, and in the United States of America at The Cooper Hewitt Museum, New York.

EXHIBITIONS INCLUDE:
1978   The Cartoon Gallery, London (solo)
1991   *The Art of The Spectator* (with Nicholas Garland), The Cartoon Gallery, London

PUBLICATIONS
Publishes regularly in *The Times,* and makes cover drawings for *The Spectator.* Has also appeared in *The Sunday Times, The Sunday Times Magazine, The Guardian, New Society, New Statesman & Society, New Scientist, Time, L'Expansion, The Times Literary Supplement, The Listener,* and *Radio Times.*

Stephen Dixon

b. 1957, Peterlee, County Durham
Studied: University of Newcastle-upon-tyne (Fine Art),
and The Royal College of Art, London (Ceramics)
Lives in Summerseat, Nr. Bury
Visiting Lecturer in Ceramics, Staffordshire
Polytechnic 1988-90, and part-time Lecturer in
Ceramics, Berkshire College of Art 1987-91.

RECENT EXHIBITIONS

1987   *Trouble in Paradise and Other Stories*, Anatol
        Orient, London (solo)
        R.C.A. in Japan, touring exhibition
1989   *The Four Continents*, Michaelson and Orient,
        London (solo)
        New English Ceramics, Sandhausen, Germany
        New Faces, Victoria and Albert Museum,
        London
1990   *Telling Tales*, Artsite Gallery, Bath
1992   *The Seven Deadly Sins*, Pro-Art, St. Louis (solo)
        Arts & Crafts to Avant-Garde, The South Bank
        Centre, London

COMMISSIONS INCLUDE:

1990   'Poll Tax' piece for the Cleveland Craft
        Collection

Jacky Fleming

b. 1955, London
Studied: Chelsea School of Art, London, and Leeds
University (Fine Art)
Lives in Leeds

RECENT EXHIBITIONS

1991   *Le Donne Ridono*, IV Biennale dell'Urismo,
        Ferrara
1992   *She Bites - Cartoons by Women*, Eastthorpe
        Gallery

PUBLICATIONS

November 1978, First published in *Spare Rib*
1983   *Women Draw* 1984 (contributor), Women's
        Press
1991   *Take a Firm Stand* (illustrations), Virago
        authors: Vicky Grosser, Gaby Mason, Rani
        Parmar
        Jacky Fleming, *Be a Bloody Train Driver*,
        Penguin Books
1992   Jacky Fleming, *Never Give Up*, Penguin Books

Cards published by Leeds Postcards, Statics
Also published by BBC, Longman, Aberdeen University
Press, The Newborne Group, and others.

Mona Hatoum

b. 1952, Beirut, Lebanon
Studied: Beirut University College, Beirut; The Byam
Shaw School of Art, and The Slade School of Art,
London
Has lived in London since 1975
Artist Residences: Western Front Art Centre,
Vancouver; 9.1.1 Contemporary Arts Centre, Seattle;
and Chisenhale Dance Space, London. Has been a part-
time lecturer at St. Martin's School of Art, London,
and Visual Arts Advisor for Greater London Arts.
Currently Senior Fellow in Fine Art, Cardiff Institute
of Higher Education, and member of editorial
advisory committee, *Third Text*.
Exhibited installations and worked particularly in
performance and video during the 1980s with many
presentations being made in Europe, Canada, and the
United States of America.

RECENT EXHIBITIONS

1990   *The British Art Show 1990*, McLellan Galleries,
          Glasgow; Leeds City Art Gallery; Hayward
          Gallery, London
          New Art for Newcastle, as part of *TSWA Four
          Cities Project*, Newcastle
1991   *Shocks to the System*, The South Bank Centre,
          London, and tour
          Interrogating Identity, Grey Art Gallery, New
          York, and tour of USA
          The Interrupted Life, The New Museum of
          Contemporary Art, New York
1992   *"Pour la Suite du Monde"*, Musée d'Art
          Contemporain de Montréal

Peter Kennard

b. 1949, London
Studied: The Byam Shaw School of Art, The Slade
School of Art, and The Royal College of Art, London
Lives in London
Exhibited widely since 1968. Photomontages
published in many newspapers and journals, and
regularly in *The Guardian*.

RECENT EXHIBITIONS

1989   *Photomontages for Peace*, United Nations,
          Palais des Nations, Geneva
1990   *Images for the End of the Century* (installation),
          Gimpel Fils Gallery, London (solo)
          Images for the End of the Century
          (photomontages), Imperial War Museum,
          London, and Fruitmarket Gallery,
          Edinburgh (solo)
1991   *Shocks to the System*, The South Bank Centre,
          London, and tour
          Photomontage Now, Manchester City
          Art Gallery
1992   Kent Gallery, New York (solo)

FILMS AND VIDEOS INCLUDE:

1983   Photomontage for Labour Party Election
          Broadcast
          Photomontage Today – Peter Kennard,
          Rodrigues, C, & Stoneman , R, (dirs.), 35mins,
          Arts Council of Great Britain
1987   *The People's Flag*, (animated montage
          sequences), Platform Films for Channel 4

RECENT PUBLICATIONS INCLUDE:

1985   Peter Kennard, *Target London* (set of
          photomontages), GLC
1990   Peter Kennard, *Images for the End of the
          Century*, Journeyman/Pluto Press

Karen Knorr

b. 1954, Frankfurt am Main, Germany
Studied: Saint John's Prep., Condado, Puerto Rico;
Franconia College, Franconia, New Hampshire;
American College, L'Atelier, and Ecole des Beaux Arts,
Paris; Harrow College of Art and Design; Polytechnic
of Central London (Film and Photographic Arts); and
Derbyshire College of Higher Education
(Photographic Studies)
Lives in London
Since 1982 freelance photographer and has been
Visiting Lecturer at Bath College of Art, Byam Shaw
School of Art, Derbyshire College of Higher Education,
Exeter College of Art and Design, Farnham College of
Art and Design, Goldsmith's College, Sir John Cass
School of Art, and Ravensbourne College of Art.
Currently Lecturer in Contemporary Photographic
Practice, London College of Printing.
Exhibited widely since 1978 in Europe, Australia,
Canada, and the United States of America.

RECENT EXHIBITIONS

1990   *Vues de l'Esprit, Photographies,* Galerie le
        Lieu, L'Orient (solo)
        *Now for the Future, Purchases for the Arts
        Council Collection since 1984,* Hayward
        Gallery, London
        Heritage, Impressions Gallery, York, and
        Cornerhouse, Manchester
        *Images in Transition: Photographic
        Representation in the 1980s,* The National
        Museum of Modern Art, Kyoto, and
        The National Museum of Modern Art, Tokyo
        El Documentalismo Social, Fotobienal, Vigo
1991   *Shocks to the System,* The South Bank Centre,
        London, and tour
        Capital, Salama-Caro Gallery, London (solo)
        Connoisseurs and Capital, Galeria 57, Madrid
        (solo)

*Gentlemen, Country Life, Connoisseurs, and
Capital,* Antoine Candau Gallery, Paris (solo)
Capital, Portfolio Gallery, Edinburgh (solo)
1992   *The Fortune Teller:* Karen Knorr, Lorna
        Simpson, Olivier Richon, Rochdale Art
        Gallery (catalogue includes details of
        exhibitions and bibliography)

Ingrid Pollard
b. 1953, Georgetown, Guyana
Studied: London College of Printing (Film & Video)
Has lived in London since 1956
Currently freelance photographer and teacher.
Exhibited widely in Britain since 1984 and also in the
United States of America.

RECENT EXHIBITIONS:
1990   *In the Ring,* CEPA Gallery, New York
        Women in my Life, Gunnersbury Museum,
        London, and tour
        Heritage, Image & History, Impressions
        Gallery, York, and tour
        'Let the Canvas come to Life with Black Faces',
        Herbert Gallery, Bristol, and tour
        Disputed Identities, Camerawork, San
        Fransisco
1991   *Interrogating Identity,* Grey Art Gallery, New
        York, and tour of USA
        Beyond Landscape, Derby Fotofest, Derby
        Stolen Glances, Stills Gallery, Edinburgh, and
        tour of UK and USA
1992   *Foto Fest,* Houston, Texas
        Women's Perspective, Bookworks Gallery,
        London
        Mai de la Photofest, Reims
        Oceans Apart (installation), Art in General,
        New York
        Fusion, Photofusion, London
        The Critical Decade, Museum of Modern Art,
        Oxford, and CAVE, Birmingham

Commissions in 1992: BBC Billboard Art Project,
London, and En Foco Inc., New York

RECENT PUBLICATIONS:
1990   *Passion,* Urban Fox Press
1991   *Stolen Glances,* Only Women Press

Chris Riddell
b. 1962, Cape Town, South Africa
Studied: Epsom School of Art & Design, and Brighton
Polytechnic Art School (Illustration)
Lives in Brighton

WRITTEN AND ILLUSTRATED CHILDREN'S BOOKS:
1985   *Ben and the Bear,* Walker Books
        Mr. Underbed, Andersen Press
1986   *The Fibbs,* Walker Books
        Bird's New Shoes, Andersen Press
1987   *The Trouble with Elephants,* Walker Books
1988   *When the Walrus Comes,* Walker Books
1989   *The Bear Dance,* Faber & Faber
1990   *The Wish Factory,* Walker Books

1988-   Political cartoonist on *The Economist*
1989-90 Political cartoonist on *The Sunday
         Correspondent*
1990-91 Business cartoonist on *The Observer*
1991-   Political cartoonist on *The Independent* and
         The Independent on Sunday
         Business cartoonist on *The Independent on
         Sunday*

Gerald Scarfe

b. 1936, London
Studied: The Royal College of Art, London
Lives in London
Made drawing for *Punch* magazine and *Private Eye* in the late fifties and early sixties. 1966 joined the *Daily Mail* as political cartoonist. Made on-the-spot drawings in Vietnam. 1967 joined the *Sunday Times* as political cartoonist; made reportage drawings in Northern Ireland, covered the Six Day War in the Middle East, and the cholera epidemic in Calcutta. 1968 worked for *Time* magazine, New York.

EXHIBITIONS
Exhibited sculpture and drawings in the late sixties including at Waddell Gallery, New York; Sears Vincent Price Gallery, Chicago; and the Pavilion d'Humeur, Montréal. Exhibited widely since then, with two recent exhibitions at Chris Beetles Gallery, London, 1988 and 1989.

THEATRE
Designed for the theatre in UK and USA since the sixties. Recent work includes:

1989   *Orpheus in the Underworld* (costumes and sets), Offenbach, English National Opera, London, and tour to Detroit, Houston, and Los Angeles

1990   *Born Again* (costumes and sets), musical written and directed by Peter Hall, Chichester Memorial Theatre

1992   *The Magic Flute* (costumes and sets), Mozart directed by Peter Hall, Los Angeles Opera House.

FILM
Worked with the Pink Floyd rock group since 1980, including design and animation for the film *Pink Floyd, The Wall*.

Directed television films since 1971, including BAFTA winner, *Scarfe by Scarfe*, 1987; *Scarfe's Follies*, 1988; *Max Miller, I like the Girls that Do*, 1989; currently working on a series of six films for BBC2 under the title: *Scarfe on:* (subjects so far shown: *Art* and *Sex*).

RECENT PUBLICATIONS BY THE ARTIST:
1986   *Scarfe by Scarfe,* Hamish Hamilton
1987   *Scarfe's Seven Deadly Sins,* Hamish Hamilton
1988   *Scarfe's Line of Attack,* Hamish Hamilton
1989   *Scarfeland,* Hamish Hamilton

Spitting Image

Spitting Image emerged from the plasticine caricatures built by Luck & Flaw for a range of magazines and newspapers, from the *New York Times* to the *Radio Times*. To see their creations move, and in desperation to make a living, they took the plunge into television, and the first show appeared in 1984. Eight years later, co-founder Roger Law has evolved from irresponsible anarchist to fat capitalist. He now presides over the world's only satire factory – a motley crew of artists, writers, directors and producers, all dedicated to taking the piss out of the rich and famous, whether on TV, in print, or ceramics.

Ralph Steadman

b. 1936, Wallasey, Cheshire
Studied: East Ham Technical College and London
College of Printing and Graphic Arts
Lives in Loose Valley
Freelance cartoonist and illustrator, has worked for
Punch magazine, *Private Eye*, and *The Daily Telegraph*
during the 1960s. Artist in Residence, University of
Sussex, 1967, and worked for The National Theatre
in 1977. Worked for *Rolling Stone* magazine through
1970s with Hunter S Thompson covering the political
scene. Illustrated many books since the sixties.

WRITTEN AND ILLUSTRATED BOOKS INCLUDE:

1979	*Sigmund Freud*, Paddington Press
1980	*The Threshold*, by Ted Hughes, Steam Press
1981	*The Curse of Lono*, Pan Picador and Bantam Books, USA
1983	*I Leonardo*, Jonathan Cape and Summit Books, USA
1986	*Paranoids*, Harrap Ltd.
1987	*Scar Strangled Banger*, book of American drawings, Harrap Ltd
1988	*The Big I Am*, Jonathan Cape
1989	*No Room to swing a Cat*, Andersen Press *America*, reprint, Fantagraphics Books, USA (originally published by Straight Arrow Books 1974)
1990	*Near the Bone*, Arrow Books *Weirrd*, Jonathan Cape
1992	*The Grapes of Ralph*, wine according to Ralph Steadman, Ebury Press

Also written the Libretto, *The Plague and the Moonflower*,
an eco-opera for the '90s, music by Richard Harvey,
for the Exeter Festival, and St Paul's Cathedral,
London, 1989, Canterbury Cathedral, 1990

RECENT EXHIBITIONS:

1989	*Who? Me? No! Why?*, Tricycle Theatre, London
1990	*Red Alert*, October Gallery, London
1991	*Raw*, Gulf War paintings, October Gallery, London

Trog (Wally Fawkes)

b. 1924, Vancouver, Canada
Studied: Sidcup Art School and Camberwell College
of Art, London
Has lived in Britain since 1931
Working as a political cartoonist he has contributed
to: *The Spectator*, *Private Eye*, *Punch*, the *New Statesman &
Society*, *The Observer*, the *Daily Mail*, *Today*, and the
London Daily News.
Also the creator of the comic strip, 'Flook'.
Wally Fawkes is also a jazz musician, playing the
clarinet, and for several years was a member of the
Humphrey Lyttleton band.

Bill Woodrow

b. 1948, near Henley-on-Thames, Oxfordshire
Studied: Winchester School of Art; St. Martins School
of Art, and Chelsea School of Art, London
Lives in London
First solo exhibition at the Whitechapel Art Gallery,
London, 1972, and then at the Kunstlerhaus
Hamburg, 1979. Since then has exhibited widely in
Europe, Brazil, Canada, United States of America, and
Australia, with regular exhibitions at Lisson Gallery,
London; Barbara Gladstone Gallery, New York; Galerie
Paul Maenz, Cologne.

RECENT EXHIBITIONS INCLUDE:
1986   Fruitmarket Gallery, Edinburgh (solo)
1987   *Documenta 8, Kassel*
1988   *Starlit Waters*, Tate Gallery, Liverpool (solo)
1989-90 *Point of Entry*, Imperial War Museum,
         London (solo)
1991   *Metropolis*, Martin Gropius Bau, Berlin
         XXI Bienal Internacional de São Paulo, (British
         Representative) São Paulo
1992   *Arte Amazonas*, Museu de Arte Moderna,
         Rio de Janiero, Brazil

List of Works

Works are listed by artist in chronological order.
Dimensions: height precedes width, which precedes
depth.
Page references for illustrations are given in brackets.

Fanny Adams

1 *Advertisement* 1992 (p. 72)
photographic enlargement
Courtesy the artists

2 *Miscellaneous publications* 1992 (p. 73)
Courtesy the artists

Art & Language

3 *Hostage XIX* 1989 (p. 63)
text on paper, glass,
oil on canvas on wood
183.4 x 122 cm
Collection the artists

4 *Hostage XXI* 1989
glass, oil on canvas on wood
183.4 x 122cm
Courtesy Lisson Gallery, London

5 *Hostage XLVI* 1990 (col. p. 64)
glass, oil on canvas on wood
183.4 x 122cm
Courtesy Lisson Gallery, London

6 *Hostage XLVIII* 1990 (col. p. 65)
glass, oil on canvas on wood
183.4 x 122cm
Courtesy Lisson Gallery, London

Steve Bell

7 *I Vow to Thee My Country* 3 June 1988 (col. p. 16)
partly after Holman Hunt
watercolour on paper, 27 x 20.2cm
Collection the artist

8 *Botha as Julius Streicher* 13 June 1988 (col. p. 17)
after John Heartfield
watercolour on paper, 13.5 x 20.2cm
Pub. *New Statesman & Society*
Collection the artist

9 *Straight-jacket, St. Francis of Assisi* 30 October 1989
acrylic on paper, 13.5 x 20.2cm
Pub. *New Statesman & Society*
Collection the artist

10 *The Tigress* 1990
watercolour on paper, 13.5 x 20.2cm
Pub. *New Statesman & Society*
Collection Kipper Williams

11 *The Three Greases* 1990
watercolour on paper, 16.5 x 25cm
from the calendar *Bell's Big Bold Bimbos* 1991
Pub. *Methuen*
Collection the artist

12 *Untitled* November 1990
ink on paper, 17.5 x 35.5cm
Pub. *The Guardian*
Collection the artist

13 *Son of Kong* December 1990
ink on paper, two sheets, images 34 x 27.5cm
and 34 x 26.6cm
Pub. *Weekend Guardian*
Collection the artist

14 *Kicks Butt* January 1991
ink on paper, 14 x 26.6cm
Pub. *The Guardian*
Collection the artist

15 *Off-shore Sharks* 7 August 1991
ink on paper, 14 x 26.6cm
Pub. *The Guardian*
Collection the artist

16 *Don't let Labour wreck the wreckage* 25 February 1992
ink on paper, 14 x 26.6cm
Pub. *The Guardian*
Collection the artist

17 *Ascent of Man* 3 March 1992 (p. 14)
ink on paper, 14 x 26.6cm
Pub. *The Guardian*
Collection the artist

18 *Cannon and Queen* 12 March 1992
ink on paper, 14 x 26.6cm
Pub. *The Guardian*
Collection the artist

19 *They're Off* 17 March 1992
ink on paper, 14 x 26.6cm
Pub. *The Guardian*
Collection the artist

20 *Punishing Times* 18 March 1992
ink on paper, 14 x 26.6cm
Pub. *The Guardian*
Collection the artist

21 *Major is a Gherkin* 20 March 1992
ink on paper, 14 x 26.6cm
Pub. *The Guardian*
Collection the artist

22 *Major as Bomb* 24 March 1992
ink on paper, 27 x 13.2cm
Pub. *The Guardian*
Collection the artist

23 *Goebbels* 26 March 1992
ink on paper, 14 x 26.6cm
Pub. *The Guardian*
Collection the artist

24 *Negative Campaign* 31 March 1992
ink on paper, 14 x 26.6cm
Pub. *The Guardian*
Collection the artist

25 *We rule you we fool you...* 11 April 1992
ink on paper, 19 x 35.2cm
Pub. *The Guardian*
Collection the artist

26 *Kinnock Banished* 14 April 1992
ink on paper, 27 x 13.2cm
Pub. *The Guardian*
Collection the artist

27 - 60 *If* 1992
34 sequences from the strip cartoon
ink on paper, each 6 x 17.5cm or 6 x 19cm*
Pub. *The Guardian*
Collection the artist
18 - 21 February
9 - 13 March
14 March*
15 - 21 March (16, 17, & 19 March p. 15)
23 - 28 March
30 March - 3 April
4 April*
13 - 17 April
18 April*

61 *Authentische Reichsfoto* 7 July 1992
ink, watercolour, and photomontage on paper,
14 x 26.8cm
Collection the artist

Peter Brookes

62 *Reagan and the Banana Republics*
12 February 1981 (p. 27)
ink on paper, 30.4 x 20.2cm
Pub. *The Listener*
Courtesy the artist

63 *Neil Kinnock* 31 May 1986
watercolour and bodycolour on paper, 18 x 26.3cm
Pub. *The Spectator*
Courtesy the artist

64 *The Press and the Law* 16 January 1988
watercolour and bodycolour on paper, 20.2 x 29.5cm
Pub. *The Spectator*
Courtesy the artist

65 *The Swing after Fragonard* July 1988
watercolour and bodycolour on paper, 35.7 x 28cm
Pub. *The Spectator*
Courtesy the artist

66 *Northern Ireland* c.1988
ink on paper, 20.7 x 22.9cm
Pub. *The Times*
Courtesy the artist

67 *Spot the Difference* 10 February 1990
watercolour and bodycolour on paper, 21.4 x 31.2 cm
Pub. *The Spectator*
Courtesy the artist

68 *Chancellor Helmut Kohl* 24 February 1990
watercolour and bodycolour on paper, 20.3 x 30 cm
Pub. *The Spectator*
Courtesy the artist

69 *Lord Denning* 18 August 1990
watercolour and bodycolour on paper, 23.6 x 35cm
Pub. *The Spectator*
Courtesy the artist

70 *Up in Smoke* 19 January 1991
watercolour and bodycolour on paper, 20.5 x 30.3cm
Pub. *The Spectator*
Private collection

71 *Wealth Bomber* 23 February 1991
watercolour and bodycolour on paper, 20.5 x 30.3cm
Pub. *The Spectator*
Courtesy the artist

72 *Lamont, after Gilray* 18 January 1992 (col. p. 29)
watercolour and bodycolour on paper, 22.9 x 33.8 cm
Pub. *The Spectator*
Courtesy the artist

73 *Chameleons* 23 March 1992 (col. p. 28)
watercolour and bodycolour on paper, 24 x 35.2cm
Pub. *The Times*
Courtesy the artist

74 *Robert Maxwell* 20 May 1992
ink on paper, 24.2 x 22.9cm
Pub. *The Times*
Courtesy the artist

75 *Major after Magritte* 22 May 1992
ink on paper, 19 x 25.3cm
Pub. *The Times*
Courtesy the artist

76 *Mostricht* 11 June 1992
ink on paper, 18 x 32.2cm
Pub. *The Times*
Collection Graham Paterson

Stephen Dixon

77 *The Nuclear Family* 1987
ceramic, 23.5 x 19.5 x 10cm
Collection Anatol Orient

78 *The City Rises* 1990 (col. p. 21)
ceramic, 35 x 30 x 30cm
Courtesy Anatol Orient

79 *Second Hand Dreams* 1990
ceramic, 28.5 x 21 x 9.5cm
Courtesy Anatol Orient

80 *Venus and Mars* 1990 (p. 19)
ceramic, 34.5 x 38 x 16cm
Courtesy Anatol Orient

81 *Death of the Lion Queen* 1991-92 (col. p. 20)
ceramic, 35.5 x 15.2 x 15.5cm
Private Collection

82 *Five More Years* 1992
ceramic, 33 x 41 x 22cm
Courtesy Anatol Orient

Jacky Fleming

83 - 99 from *Be a Bloody Train Driver* 1991 (p. 42-45)
17 drawings from the book
originals: ink on paper
copies exhibited, each 21.3 x 29.7cm
Pub. *Penguin Books*, October 1991
Courtesy the artist

100 - 102 from *Never Give Up* 1992
3 drawings from the book
originals: ink on paper
copies exhibited, each 21.3 x 29.7cm
to be published by *Penguin Books*, November 1992
Courtesy the artist

Mona Hatoum

103 *Over My Dead Body* 1988 (p. 71)
Metro Billboard Project, Projects UK Newcastle
photomontage poster in six sections, 183 x 305cm
Courtesy the artist

Peter Kennard

104 *Gulf* 1991 (details p. 51)
photomontage panels, overall 275 x 730cm
Collection the artist

105 *Installation* 1973-92 (2 photomontages,
col. p. 52 & 53)
photomontages, newspapers, magazines, posters,
bookcovers, T-shirts and badges
Collection the artist

Display of work by Peter Kennard sponsored by
W Photo & W Business Presentation Limited

Karen Knorr

106 - 110 *Connoisseurs*
5 cibachromes mounted on museum board, brass
plaques with text on black ramin frames,
each 88.9 x 91.4cm
Collection the artist and
•Collection Chase Manhattan Bank

The Genius of the Place 1986, 1/5 •
Looking at Great Works of Art 1989, 3/5 (p. 59)
The Libertine Manner of Reading 1986, 3/5
Pleasures of the Imagination 1986, 2/5
Thoughts on the Imitation of Ideas 1986, Artist's Proof

111 - 116 *Capital*
6 cibachromes, mounted on museum board with
gold leaf lettering on brown ramin frames,
each 103.3 x 103.3cm
Collection the artist

The End of History 1992 2/5 (col. p. 61)
His Worshipful Company 1990, 2/5
Liquid Assets 1991, 2/5 (col. p. 60)
The Mile on the Square 1990, 2/5
First World Debts 1990, 2/5
Principles of Political Economy 1991, 2/5

Ingrid Pollard

117 *A Trip to Hastings* 1991-92 (details, p. 55 - 57)
14 panels with photographs, text and mixed media,
each 55.9 x 40.6cm
Collection the artist

Chris Riddell

118 *Greater Serbia* 25 November 1991 (p. 30)
ink on paper, 29.6 x 49cm
Collection the artist

119 *Opt Out* 2 December 1991 (col. p. 33)
ink on paper, 29.6 x 49cm
Collection the artist

120 *Benetton Wolf* 27 January 1992 (p. 31)
ink on paper, 29.6 x 49cm
Collection the artist

121 *South African Referendum* 16 March 1992
ink on paper, 29.6 x 49cm
Collection the artist

122 *Labour Havoc* 30 March 1992
ink on paper, 29.6 x 49cm
Collection the artist

123 *Royal Press Coverage* 17 May 1992
ink on paper, 51 x 29.6cm
Collection the artist

124 *Earth Summit* 31 May 1992
ink on paper, 51 x 29.6cm
Collection the artist

125 *White Elephant* 1 June 1992
ink on paper, 29.6 x 49cm
Collection the artist

126 *Slob* 2 June 1992
ink on paper, 29.6 x 49cm
Collection the artist

127 *Danish No Vote* 4 June 1992
ink on paper, 29.6 x 49cm
Collection the artist

128 *Baroness Thatcher* 8 June 1992
ink on paper, 29.6 x 49cm
Collection Timothy Lane

129 *Oftel Watchdog* 10 June 1992
ink on paper, 29.6 x 49cm
Collection the artist

130 *Re-election Logging* 12 June 1992
ink on paper, 29.6 x 49cm
Collection the artist

131 *Cultural Weapons* 22 June 1992 (p. 32)
ink on paper, 29.6 x 49cm
Collection the artist

Gerald Scarfe

132 - 143 *Who's to Blame?* c.1988 - 92
(p. 34 & 35 and col. p. 36 & 37) 12 pen, ink, and
watercolour drawings on paper, each 84 x 60cm
Pub. *The Sunday Times*
Collection the artist

Spitting Image

144 *The Last Supper* 1992
after Leonardo da Vinci
installation
Created by Spitting Image
(works by Luck and Flaw and Spitting Image are
illustrated, p. 11 & col. p. 12 and 13)

Barbican Art Gallery acknowledges with thanks the
support of Central TV for *Spitting Image* installation.
Photographic enlargements sponsored by W Photo &
W Business Presentations Limited

Ralph Steadman

145 *Show of Hands* c.1971
photomontage on paper, 35 x 48cm
Collection the artist

146 *City in 2002* 1977
photomontage and drawing, 56 x 80cm
Collection the artist

147 *In The Beginning* May 1979
drawing on newsprint, 39 x 33cm
Pub. *New Statesman & Society*
Collection the artist

148 *Electronic Earth Hug* 1979
photomontage and ink on paper, 57 x 56cm
Pub. *New Statesman & Society*
Collection the artist

149 *One-balled World* 1979
ink on paper, 57 x 80cm
Pub. *New Statesman & Society*
Collection the artist

150 *Frankenstein's Real Estate* c.1981 (col.p. 48)
photomontage and inks on paper, 90 x 59cm
Collection the artist

151 *Consumer Crucifix* c.1982
photomontage and ink on paper, 70 x 54cm
Collection the artist

152 *The Adoration of the Maggie* 1983 (p. 47)
ink on paper, 59 x 84cm
Pub. *New Statesman & Society*
Collection the artist

153 *The Smile* 1984
photomontage and ink on paper, 59 x 53cm
Pub. *New York Times*
Collection the artist

154 *Paranoids: World Leaders* 1986
15 Polaroids, each 8.8 x 10.7cm
Collection the artist

155 *Paranoids: Kinnock etc.* 1986
16 Polaroids, each 8.8 x 10.7cm
Collection the artist

156 *Paranoids: Maggie etc.* 1986
21 Polaroids, each 8.8 x 10.7cm
Collection the artist

157 *Gulf* 1991
two triptychs and six single sheets
photomontages with mixed media on paper
each sheet 85 x 65cm
Collection the artist

Smart Bomb (triptych)
Jingo Art (triptych)
Tower of Babel (col. p. 49)
Scrapheap
Disconsulate Carrier
Deadly Calculation
Love Child - Hug
Gas Mask

158 *The Morning After* April 1992
ink on paper, 20 x 41.5cm
Pub. *The Guardian*
Collection the artist

159 *Help Arlington House* 1992
photomontage and ink on paper, 64.8 x 55cm
design for T-shirt
Collection the artist

160 *Earth Summit* 1992
ink and watercolour on paper, 62 x 46cm
design for Friends of the Earth poster
Collection the artist

161 *The Hollow Suit* June 1992
(cover and details p. 1 & 96)
photomontage and mixed media, 89.9 x 70cm
design for *The Cutting Edge* exhibition poster
Collection the artist

Trog (Wally Fawkes)

162 *Untitled* 8 June 1986 (p. 24)
ink on paper, 16.9 x 38.3cm
Pub. *The Observer*
Courtesy the artist

163 *Untitled* 1990 (p. 22)
ink on paper, 21 x 30.3cm
Pub. *The Observer*
Courtesy the artist

164 *Untitled* 14 July 1991 (p. 25)
ink on paper, 21 x 30.5cm
Pub. *The Observer*
Courtesy the artist

165 *Untitled* 28 July 1991
ink on paper, 21.5 x 31.5cm
Pub. *The Observer*
Courtesy the artist

166 *Untitled* 8 December 1991 (p. 23)
ink on paper, 21 x 30.5cm
Pub. *The Observer*
Courtesy the artist

167 *Untitled* 22 December 1991
ink on paper, 21 x 30.5cm
Pub. *The Observer*
Courtesy the artist

168 *Untitled* 29 December 1991
ink on paper, 21 x 30.5cm
Pub. *The Observer*
Courtesy the artist

169 *Untitled* 19 January 1992
ink on paper, 21 x 30.5cm
Pub. *The Observer*
Courtesy the artist

170 *Untitled* 31 May 1992
ink on paper, 21 x 30.5cm
Pub. *The Observer*
Courtesy the artist

Bill Woodrow
171 *Endeavour (cannon dredged from the first wreck of the 'Ship of Fools')* 1990 (p. 67 & 68, details, and col. p. 69)
cardboard maquette, 208 x 445 x 174cm
Courtesy the artist

Index

Published August 1992 in an edition of 1,500 copies
on the occasion of Barbican Art Gallery's exhibition:
The Cutting Edge
13 August - 18 October 1992

Exhibition selected and organised by Carol Brown
and John Hoole with assistance from Donna Loveday
and Clare Stent

Catalogue edited by Carol Brown
Designed by Arefin Coates
Typeset by Quest
Printed by EGA, Brighton

cover: Ralph Steadman *The Hollow Suit* 1992 (Cat. 161)
details p. 1 & 96

ISBN 0 946372 26 8

PHOTOGRAPHY ACKNOWLEDGEMENTS
We wish to thank the artists and the following:
Courtesy British Film Institute *p. 39, 40, 41*
Jonthan Morris Ebbs *p. 19, 20, 21, 28, 29, 36 - 37, 47 - 49,
56, 57*
John Lawrence Jones *p. 12, 13*
Courtesy Luck and Flaw *p. 11*
Courtesy Fergal McAleer *p. 52*
Sue Omerod *p. 64, 65*
Gareth Winters *p. 63*
Edward Woodman *p. 71*